Written by VA RIVERA

KIDS READ AND WRITE SERIES BOOK #3

CREATIVE COUPLETS

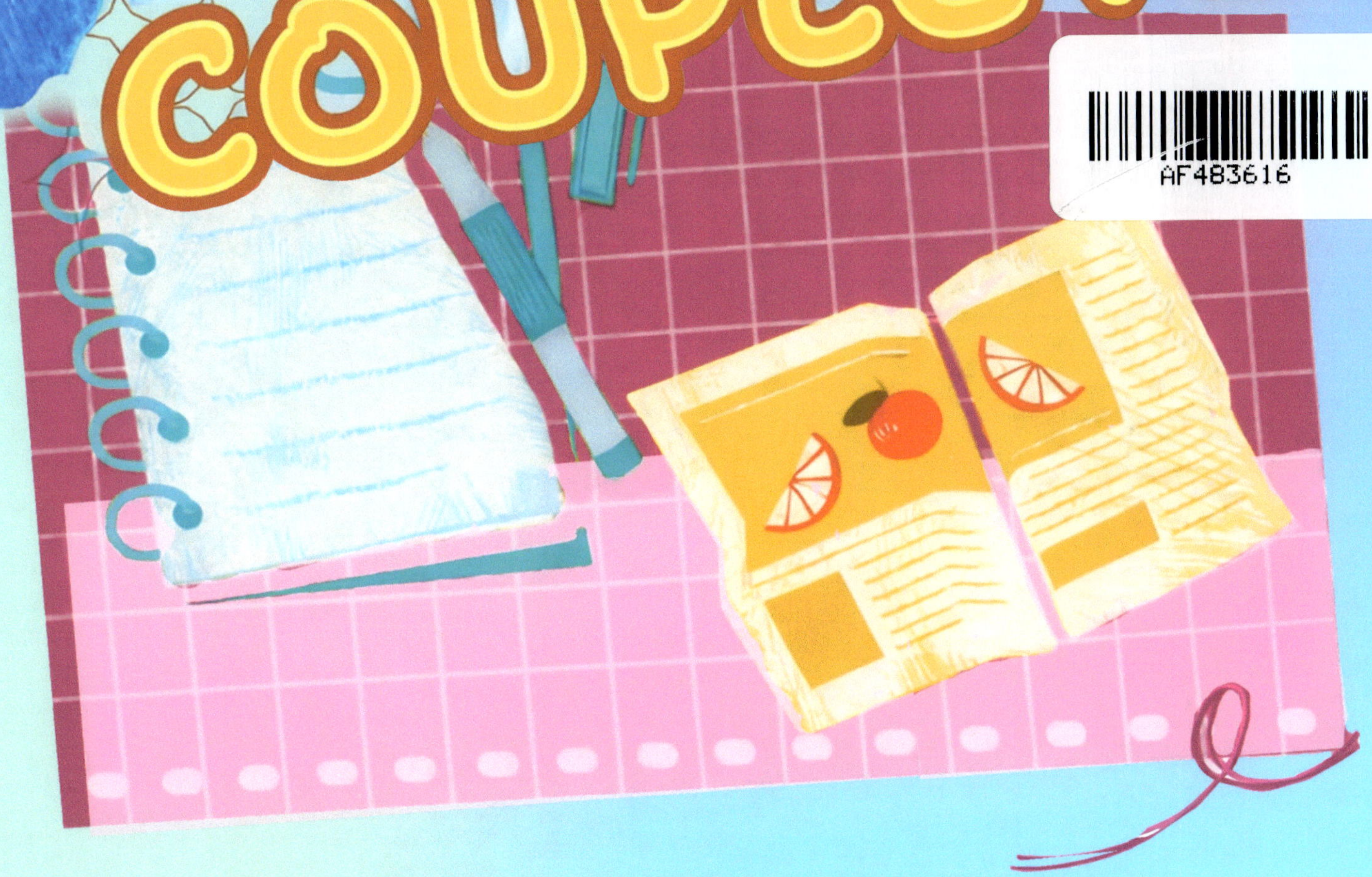

When kids know how to write Couplet poems, there is no stopping them! Once again, VA Rivera recognizes the poet within every child. Ms. Rivera encourages kids to express their thoughts and ideas in writing clever, serious, heartfelt, or even funny Couplets.

Go get 'em, Kids!

VA RIVERA
Poetry Workshops
va_rivera@varivera.com
https://www.varivera.com

Table Of Contents

INTRODUCTION

Kids have fun with a crayon, pencil, or pen

A sticky note, notebook, and pencil can be a best friends

Ideas that kids can write could change the world

Imagine the stories just waiting to be unfurled.

Rhymes, ideas, and thoughts may soon arise

Envision a better life through a child's eyes

So pick up your tools, with imagination in flight

Your words are a light to make your future

grow bright.

Welcome to a World of Couplets!  

Kids can have fun with Couplets, making them clever, serious, or even funny. When kids know how to write the form of a Couplet, there is no stopping them.

Bright young minds are filled with new ideas and innovative ways of thinking. Kids can use their ideas for creative writing. Poetry is a form of creative writing that kids master. With no hard and fast rules, poems are simple enough for the youngest child, while at the same time, challenging enough for a young adult or even a seasoned writer.

KIDS!

Come along on a journey of writing Couplet poems. If you yearn to be creative, today is only the start for the budding poet within your soul ...

BECAUSE EVERY CHILD CAN CREATE A POEM

Let's Get Started with a Warm-Up:

Think of the word that makes sense in the blanks:

i.   When you think of two persons, you are thinking of a c_________ of people.

ii.   When you think of two things, you are thinking of a co_______ of things.

iii.   When you think of two places, you are thinking of a cou______ of places.

PEOPLE:

Two parents are a _________e of parents,

Two children are a ________le of children,

Two nurses are a _______ple of nurses

►Look around for a couple of people. List the couple's names!

____

____

PLACES:

Two Art rooms are a _____________ of Art rooms.

Two Burger Restaurants are a ____of Burger Restaurants.

Two playgrounds are a _____ ____ of playgrounds.

►Look around for a couple of places. List the places.

THINGS:

Two pencils are a ________________ of pencils.

Two dolls are a ________________ of dolls.

Two soccer balls are a ________________ soccer balls.

►Look around for a couple of things. What are they?

Unscramble the letters for the answer:

P   L   O   C   E   U

A ____ ____ ____ ____ ____ ____

Try naming more couples:

1. (persons) ... a couple of _____________________

2. (places) ... a couple of _____________________

3. (things) ... a couple of _____________________

DRAWING PAGE

A COUPLE OF PENCILS

A COUPLE OF HOUSES

A COUPLE OF ORANGUTANS

NOW DRAW YOUR OWN & WRITE A LABEL

Chapter 1

ABOUT COUPLET POEMS

The Couplet form was first used in ancient Greek and Roman poetry.

The Poet, Mimnermus wrote (7th century BCE):

"Life without love is nothing but a day,

Empty of joy, and quickly fades away."

☞ Love is necessary.

Reread Mimnermus' couplet poem. Look for one characteristic you notice about the couplet.

Write what you notice:

____

The Poet, Martial wrote a collection called, Epigrams. Here is one of the Couplets:

"A little book, so small it fits your hand, Yet filled with wit that all may understand."

☞ A tiny book that is full of clever words.

(What tiny book can you think of that is full of clever words?)

Read Martial's couplet poem. Look for one characteristic you notice about the couplet.

Write what you notice:

____

Centuries later, rhyming Couplets became popular in English literature with Geoffrey Chaucer in the 14th century. He wrote a collection of short stories called

The Canterbury Tales.

Here is one of two Chaucer Couplets:

"And smale foweles maken melodye, That slepen al the nyght with open eye."

☞ Birds singing and sleeping

(Draw a bird singing while it sleeps!)

Reread Chaucer's couplet poem. Look for one characteristic you notice about the couplet?

Write what you notice:

____

Here is the second Chaucer Couplet:

"Of studie took he most cure and most heede, Noght o word spak he moore than was neede."

☞ A student studies hard while being quiet and focused.

Reread Chaucer's second couplet poem. Look for one characteristic you notice about the couplet?

Write what you notice:

____

Chaucer's rhyming couplets influenced poets such as Shakespeare, who famously used them to express many important ideas.

In *A Midsummer Night's Dream*, Shakespeare wrote about fairies singing a blessing:

"Hand in hand, with fairy grace,

Will we sing, and bless this place."

☞ Can you imagine fairies

dancing?

Reread Shakespeare's second couplet poem. Look for one characteristic you notice about the couplet?

Write what you notice:

____

In Shakespeare's *Macbeth*, witches chant

👉 Listen for a magic sing-song rhyme:

"Double, double, toil and trouble;
Fire burn and cauldron bubble."

Reread Shakespeare's second couplet poem. Look for one characteristic you notice about the couplet?

Write what you notice:

____

Chapter 2

COUPLETS TODAY

Couplets have evolved through time and across cultures, but simplicity and rhyme keep the poetic form popular even today.

Try completing the following rhyming couplets:

"The silver star is hiding in the sky,
as clouds reveal, it's floating up _____."

"The flowers dance when breezes start to sway,

They bow and laugh to end another _____."

"A gentle cat, will curl beside your feet,

she's purring songs so soft, and oh, so ________."

Find the rhyming words in all 3 of 'Today's' couplets.

Write the words here: ________ ________

________ ________

________ ________

Practice more rhyming by writing one word in each blank for the following words:

Rest _____________ Girl ___________

Fix ____________ Might ___________

Cat ____________ Heap ___________

Boy _____________ Soon ___________

Fill in the blank spaces.

HAVE FUN!

First, choose a topic:

✓ *Think of a favorite animal, pet, or other living thing.*

For Example:

BABY SPIDER

✓ <u>*NEXT, make a list of 8 words that describe your living thing.*</u>

Example words for Baby Spider:

fuzzy

Wilber's friend

____

flies

catches prey

air bubbles in water

sticky

____

✓ <u>*Write Matching Rhyming Words*</u>

fuzzy	<u>*muzzy*</u>
catches prey	<u>*today*</u>
Wilber's friend	__________
air bubbles in water	__________
__________	__________
sticky	__________
flies	__________
__________	__________

✓ **Finally, choose 2 rhyming words to write a Couplet:**

Example:

<u>*BABY* SPIDER</u> - <u>catches prey</u> today

Baby Spider quickly ______.

He's hungry, so he wants to eat _________.

>Try two more rhyming words: fuzzy & muzzy

Baby Spider is not very ________

Knowing why seems just a little ________

[FUN EXTRA: He wasn't thinking clearly, ______ ____?] ;D

Now it's your turn:

✓   *Think of a favorite animal, pet, or other living thing.*

____

✓   **NEXT, make a list of 8 words that describe your living thing.**

_____________   _____________

_____________   _____________

_____________   _____________

_____________   _____________

✓ ## <u>*Write Matching Rhyming Words*</u>

✓   Finally, choose 2 rhyming words to write a Couplet:

____________________   ____________________

Write a Couplet:

____

____

Try another Couplet:

____

____

GOOD JOB, POET!

Now you are ready for more!

Chapter 3

WHAT IS METER?

Meter in a couplet (or any poem) is like a beat in music.

It's the short and long sounds of the rhythm.

Imagine clapping along to the words—meter helps you know when to

clap! 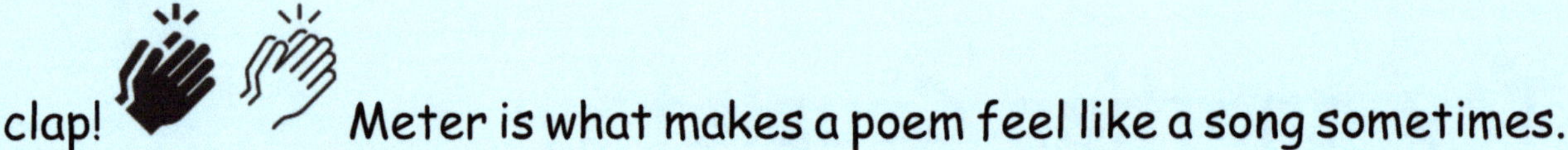 Meter is what makes a poem feel like a song sometimes.

Next, get ready to clap...

The Couplets you have read so far have a meter called Iambic Pentameter. Iambic Pentameter has 5 beats in each line. Try clapping on each beat.

Example A:

A GENtle CAT, will CURL beSIDE your FEET,
   1   2   3 4   5

PURRing SONGS so SOFT, and OH, so SWEET.
   1   2   3   4   5

Example B:

My PUPpy DOG likes CHEWing ON his BONE.
   1   2   3   4   5

WHEN he's DONE, he GOES out FOR a RUN.
   1   2   3   4   5

Example C:

At SCHOOL, my TEAcher IS the NICEst ONE.
   1   2 3   4   5

She MAKES our WORK and LEARNing LOTS of FUN.
   1   2   3   4   5

Challenge: Iambic Pentameter (five beats) is difficult, but you can do it. Try writing a rhyming couplet with 5 beats about another favorite animal, pet, or insect.

____

____

____

____

____

____

Draw a picture that matches one of your rhyming couplets:

Chapter 4

OTHER COUPLET METERS

Nursery Rhymes usually have a 3- or 4-beat meter. You may already know some of these rhyming couplets!

Clap and count the meter patterns.

What is the meter for these three couplets?

Twinkle, twinkle, little star,   (<u>4</u>)

How I wonder what you are!   (<u>4</u>)

Humpty Dumpty sat on a wall,   _____

Humpty Dumpty had a great fall.   _____

Baa, baa, black sheep, have you any wool?_____

Yes sir, yes sir, three bags full. _____

The next three couplets have mixed meter.

What do you think mixed meter means?

Clap the counts and find out!

i.   Jack and Jill went up the hill,   _____

To fetch a pail of water   _____

ii.　　　Hey diddle diddle, the cat and the fiddle, _____

The cow jumped over the moon.  _____

iii.　　　Ol' King Cole was a merry ol' soul _____

and a merry old soul was he. _____

He called for his spoon, and be called

for his bowl, _____

and he called for his fiddlers, three. _____

Chapter 5

PRACTICE WRITING COUPLET POEMS

Use the following rhyming words (or use your own rhyming words) to help you write original rhyming couplets on the lines below:

tree, knee	breathe,
seed	sun, fun
flower, power	spoon,
moon	rocket, pocket
cloud, loud	green,
seen	try, fly

____

____

CONGRATULATIONS!!!

<u>You are a Poet</u>
<u>who writes creative</u>
<u>couplet poems!</u>

??Did you know Coupets come in other forms??

Are you ready to write a new
type of Couplet?

What are Tirakkural Couplets?

Tirukkaral Couplets

(Pronounced: Thir - roo - kur - rul)

are ancient two- line Tamil*

poems with exactly 7 words.

*(Tamil is a group of people living in parts of southern India and Sri Lanka.
Tamil is also the name of the language spoken by the Tamil people.)

But how do I write a Tirukkural Couplet?

The first line of a Tirukkural
Couplet has 4 words.
The second line has 3 words

But wait,
there's more ...

A Tirukkaral Couplet
teaches a lesson about
right and wrong.

Tirukkural themes are usually Goodness, Wealth, and Love

Examples of <u>Tirukkural Couplets' Themes</u>:

Goodness:

1.   Win friends by being

     honest and true.

2.   Daily rainfall gives life

     to living things.

3.   Kind words make friends,

     harshness makes frowns

Wealth:

1. Green plants give riches

    to every creature.

2. Share your supplies and

    make someone _______.

3. Build your _______ by

    making another friend.

Love

4. In our family, love's

    the _______ gift.

5. My heart skips when

    _______ my dog.

6.   I purr like my

      kitten with ______

Now you try:

7.   Goodness

8.   Wealth

9.   Love

Does a Tirukkural (couplet) need to Rhyme?

Good question!

Rhyming Tirukkural couplets are written in the Tamil language.

However, in English, the meaning is more important than the rhyme.

Chapter 7

WRITE YOUR OWN TIRUKKURAL COUPLETS

Here's a challenge:

Use the space below to write rhyming **Tirukkural**

Couplets. Fill in the rhyming words:

1. Skunks are cute from

    far, not near

    they really stink, is

    what I _______

2. Teacher says I bounce

    like a ball

    Today I will roll

    down the _______

3. Write your own rhyming Tirukkural Couplet:

CONGRATULATIONS!!!

You are a Poet
who writes **Rhyming
Couplets** AND creative
Tirukkural Couplets!

<u>*Final Thoughts:*</u> **Rhyming Couplet** poems are fun.

Tirukkural Couplet poems are a bit more challenging. Either way, now you can write both!

Well done, my friends! Keep writing!
There is no stopping you, now!

____

____

____

____

____

____